THE
HUMAN
BODY
Questions and Answers

THOMAS CANAVAN

ARCTURUS

ARCTURUS

This edition published in 2016 by Arcturus Publishing Limited
26/27 Bickels Yard, 151–153 Bermondsey Street,
London SE1 3HA

Copyright © Arcturus Holdings Limited

Text by Thomas Canavan
Edited by Lisa Regan
Designed by Supriya Sahai

All pictures from Shutterstock including 35br Aspen Photo / Shutterstock.com; 47br MarcelClemens / Shutterstock.com; 54bl Neale Cousland /Shutterstock.com; 59tr sportpoint /Shutterstock.com; 72bl Paolo Bona / Shutterstock.com; 73tr Reinhard Tiburzy /Shutterstock.com; 99br Maxisport /Shutterstock.com; 112tl Christian Bertrand / Shutterstock.com

ISBN: 978-1-78428-220-2
CH004934NT
Supplier 26, Date 1116, Print run 5251

Printed in China

1

2

CONTENTS

3

MUSCLES AND MOVEMENT

4

YOUR VITAL ORGANS

5

CELLS AND SYSTEMS

6

SENSES AND SENSATIONS

What are humans made of?

Human bodies come in varying shapes and sizes, but on the inside we're pretty much made of the same set of parts. We belong to the vertebrate section of the animal kingdom, so we have a spine; we breathe air through our mouth, so we have lungs, and we walk the earth to find food and shelter, so we have limbs, a digestive system, and sensory organs to keep us safe.

Vertebrate

Who are you calling spineless?

Plant

Invertebrate

The **endocrine system** is in charge of growth and the chemicals that are vital for you to function properly.

Your brain is a part of the **nervous system**.

The heart pumps blood around the **circulatory system.**

The **respiratory system** is all about breathing.

Your **skeletal system** supports your body every day.

Your **nervous system** links your spinal cord and a whole network of nerves that feed information to your brain.

Super systems

Of course, that's not all we're made of. Humans are extremely complex machines with countless working parts. To make sense of these parts, biologists and doctors deal with them in groups called systems. Specialists study bones, the blood, the brain, the nerves—all of which form part of their own systems working hard inside your body.

The **digestive system** helps your body extract goodness from your food.

You can feel your **muscular system** in action each time you move.

What's inside our body?

All living things—plant or animal, vertebrate or invertebrate—are made up of cells. The bacteria that cause diseases are single-celled creatures, but humans are quite obviously much more complex. A human body has around 200 different types of cells, most of them too small to see without a microscope.

A-tissue!

Animal or plant cells with a similar function can group together to form living tissue. This tissue carries out a particular job, such as taking up water (in plants) or lining your intestine to help food move smoothly on its way. Your nose has its own lining of mucus-producing tissue, too. It prevents unwanted substances from invading your body—but if you suffer from a cold or an allergy, you produce extra, and will have to get rid of some of it!

Organ-ised

Different tissues combine to form the organs of the body, which carry out their own particular jobs inside you. Your heart, for example, contains fibrous tissue, muscle tissue, and other special cells to control how it beats. These organs can be grouped together in systems (see pages 4-5). Some items on the list of organs might surprise you: your tongue, for instance, is an organ that helps you talk, chew, taste, and swallow.

A footnote from history

It has taken many centuries for doctors to learn so much about the human body. Early societies mixed their medicine with magic, religion, and superstition. Poor hygiene and living conditions allowed diseases to spread easily. From the 1900s, doctors had machines to study the body, injections to prevent illnesses, and better knowledge of how to treat their patients. Great leaps have been made in medicine, and now we can transplant organs, make artificial body parts, and have wiped out some diseases altogether.

Someone call a doctor!

Why do we need skin and hair?

Your "outer wrappings" of skin, hair, teeth, and nails do a lot more than keep up appearances. Between them, they protect you from damage or infection and keep you at the right temperature. You can become seriously ill if you get too hot or too cold. Your skin acts as a blanket against the cold and allows heat to escape when you're hot.

Are all hairs the same thickness?

Generally speaking, East Asian people have thicker individual hairs than people from other parts of the world.

Is your hair stronger than steel?

An object of around 100 g (3 oz) could dangle on a single strand of human hair. That's nearly two regular sized bars of soap! It's not quite as strong as steel, but it's up there with other strong substances like Kevlar, used to make bulletproof vests.

Bacteria, yuck!

Why do hairs really stand on end?

Your body hairs lie flat when you're hot and rise up when you're cold to trap a warming "blanket" of air.

How does skin protect you from germs?

Think about all the germs in the air, and on the things you touch. Your skin shields your organs and major systems from the illnesses that those germs can cause. Just a small break in your skin can provide an opening for infection. That's why your body works quickly to form a scab over a cut. It plugs the hole so that new skin can grow.

How thick is your skin?

It differs in thickness around your body. The thickest skin is on the soles of your feet, and is around 4 mm (0.16 in) thick. Your eyelids are made of some of your thinnest skin, only 0.5 mm (0.02 in) thick. Your skin does lots of different jobs, from protecting and insulating your body to giving you the sense of touch.

Thinnest skin!

Is skin really an organ?

Yes—the largest of the body's organs. Laid flat, a 13-year-old's skin would cover around 1.7 m² (18 square feet)—about the size of a single bed.

Thickest skin!

How does skin work?

It is divided into layers. The bit that you can see, called the epidermis, is the outside layer. It forms the protective barrier for your body. The layer beneath is the dermis, which contains blood vessels, sweat glands, and hair follicles. The bottom layer, called the hypodermis, connects your skin with your muscles.

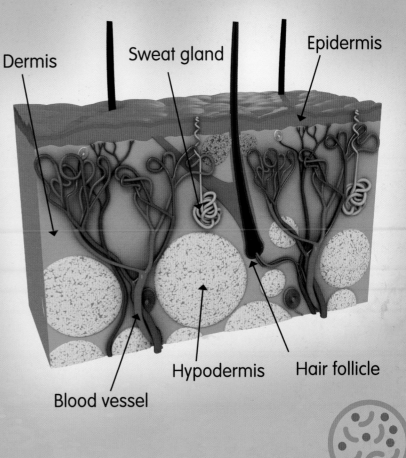

Dermis

Sweat gland

Epidermis

Hypodermis

Hair follicle

Blood vessel

How much dead skin comes off?

Every minute you lose 30,000 to 40,000 dead cells from the surface of your skin.

Yikes!

Are we really covered by dead skin?

The skin that you see is made up of dead skin cells. New cells are constantly forming at the base of the epidermis. They then begin the journey upward. Older cells, nearer the surface, die, and rise to the surface as these new cells replace them.

11

Why don't women have beards?

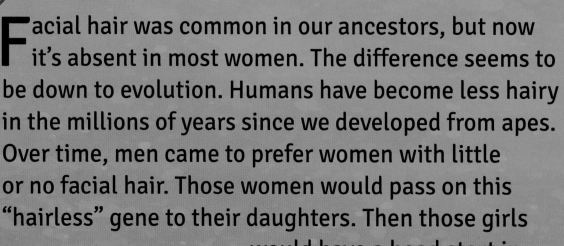

Facial hair was common in our ancestors, but now it's absent in most women. The difference seems to be down to evolution. Humans have become less hairy in the millions of years since we developed from apes. Over time, men came to prefer women with little or no facial hair. Those women would pass on this "hairless" gene to their daughters. Then those girls would have a head start in the ancient dating game.

How fast do beards grow?

Most body hair grows at the same rate: about 1.25 cm (½ inch) a month. The average man spends 60 hours shaving each year.

Why don't boys shave?

Boys' bodies begin to change as they become adults. Many of those changes are caused by hormones (chemicals produced by the body). One of those hormones, called testosterone, builds up muscles, makes boys' voices get deeper, and causes hair to begin growing on the face and on other parts of the body.

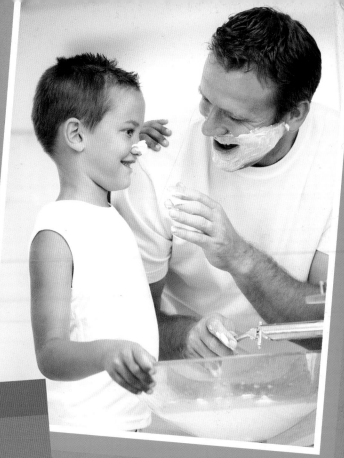

How long can a beard grow?

The longest beard ever measured stretched 5.33 m (17 ½ feet).

Why aren't the palms of our hands hairy?

Even the furriest, hairiest mammals have no hair follicles on the palms of their hands or soles of their feet. Hairs would be worn away by the constant contact with the ground, and would make it more difficult to grip onto things.

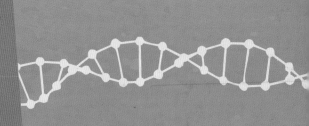

13

Why don't women go bald?

Women may not have beards, but they normally keep the hair on the top of their head all their life. For the same reason that men have beards, it's down to hormones. The male hormone testosterone can make hair follicles shrivel up until no more hair grows. Although women produce some testosterone, their female hormones protect their hair.

Keratin!

What is hair made of?

Hair is mostly made up of a protein called keratin. It is the same substance that makes your fingernails and toenails. It is also what animals' hooves, claws, horns, and even feathers and beaks are made of.

What is a follicle?

Each of your 100,000 hairs grows from its own follicle, a tiny organ in the dermis layer of your skin.

Can women ever lose their hair?

As girls mature, their bodies start to produce sex hormones that will help them have babies. These are the female hormones that protect their hair. Women stop producing sex hormones when they're too old to have babies. Their hair can become thinner, and even disappear. Some women may lose their hair completely if their hormones are affected by something out of the ordinary. That could be an illness, a shock, or even having a baby.

How long do hairs last?

The average lifespan of a human hair is 2–7 years. Then it is replaced.

Why do we have eyebrows?

Eyebrows might seem like an afterthought, added once human faces were designed. But they serve some practical purposes in protecting you. Their location just above your eyes makes them ideal guards for two of your most delicate organs. Plus—as you probably know—they are an excellent way of communicating emotions.

What if you had no eyebrows?

You can simply look at a mannequin in a department store window to see how odd you'd look. But eyebrows have an important job to do—diverting sweat, rain, and other liquids from flowing into your eyes. Together with your eyelashes, which catch dust and other objects, they protect your sense of sight.

Can eyebrows speak?

Eyebrows are an important part of non-verbal communication—the type that doesn't involve words or even sounds. Most of us can judge another person's mood by first looking at their facial expression. Eyebrows are especially good at revealing your emotions—whether you're sad, angry, happy, or surprised.

How do eyebrows move?

There are over 40 muscles in the head and face, which help you frown, smile, and raise your eyebrows in surprise.

What if you pluck your eyebrows?

Your eyebrows can grow back, but they're the slowest-growing hairs on your body.

17

Why do we get chapped lips?

Your lips lack sweat glands, so don't produce natural oils to stop them from drying out. Lips are also covered with a much thinner layer of skin than the rest of your body. This makes them more sensitive (and explains the fact that lips are usually a different shade from the rest of your face, as the blood vessels are nearer the surface).

Why do lips tingle?
There are lots of nerve endings near the surface of the skin. Lips react to some spices just as they would if they were being tickled!

How many muscles do lips use?

A simple action like blowing a trumpet uses a set of four muscles around the mouth.

Do we really need our lips to live?

One of the very first things you did—apart from crying—was to suckle, or pucker your lips to take in milk. This basic action, or instinct, allows you to get essential nourishment. Your lips continue to help you eat, sealing your mouth as you chew and swallow. They are also very sensitive to touch, which helps warn your body about danger.

My lips are sealed!

Why do lips make different shapes?

Lip muscles help you move food into your mouth and make sounds that others can hear. Your lips help you produce about half of the sounds that you need to speak. Try saying, "My big mouth," without closing your lips! They also seal your mouth closed to keep out water or dirt.

Why do we grow two sets of teeth?

It might seem odd replacing a full set of teeth, but your first set of milk (or baby) teeth has done its job by the time you're five or six years old. They've helped you chew and get important nourishment, as well as learn to talk. It's time for your body to prepare to house a larger, adult set of teeth.

CHOMP! CHOMP!

Are adult teeth tougher than baby teeth?

No, they're just bigger! Your 20 milk teeth do their job very well, allowing you to slice, cut, and grind food. But you need more teeth to fill your larger, adult jaw. The first set helps your jaw grow in a way that will let your second set replace that first set—and still have room for the 12 extra teeth that adults have.

What are wisdom teeth?

Most people also have a third set of teeth—four molars called "wisdom teeth" that arrive when you're about 20.

Tough AND wise, huh?!

How does your first set know when to fall out?

That second set of teeth starts to develop while your first set is in place. When they're ready, they push through the jaw. Along the way, they dissolve the roots of the first set. Without those roots to anchor them, the milk teeth become loose.

What makes teeth so strong?

The outer layer of your teeth is covered in enamel, the hardest tissue in your body.

21

What causes toothache?

Toothache is a sign that something is wrong inside or near one of your teeth. It's mainly the result of dental decay—bits of a tooth being eaten away allowing germs to get inside. Luckily you can reduce the chance of developing a toothache with good habits like regular daily brushing.

How serious is toothache?

Severe tooth decay can kill you! Historians believe that ancient Egypt's Pharaoh Ramesses II died of toothache.

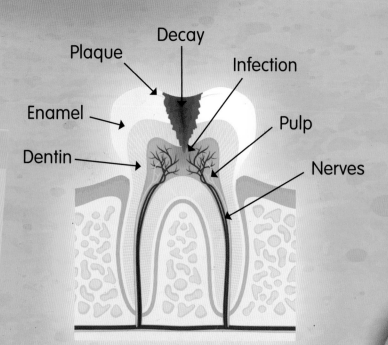

Plaque

Decay

Infection

Enamel

Pulp

Dentin

Nerves

Why is toothache so painful?

Plaque, a sticky substance containing lots of bacteria, constantly forms around your teeth. Sugars from food mix with the bacteria, releasing acid. It can eat through the outer layer of your teeth and cause cavities, or holes. Germs enter through these cavities, eating away at the inside of your teeth. The pain is a signal from the nerves in the affected area.

What if an adult tooth falls out?

If it gets knocked out whole, a dentist may be able to set it back in place. Keep it in milk and get it looked at immediately.

How can we prevent toothache?

Regular brushing helps prevent germs from collecting and attacking your teeth. And you should try not to have too many sugary foods or drinks because they can eat away at the enamel covering of your teeth, opening the way for painful infection.

23

Why don't humans have claws?

What are the white spots on nails?

Small white marks are no big deal—you may have knocked or bent the nail. But nails can show how healthy you are—if they're darker or have patches on them, you might be unwell.

Most mammals have sharp claws to help them dig or to attack other animals. Primates, the group of mammals that includes monkeys, apes, and humans, have nails instead. As primates developed, claws became smaller and flatter. These smaller versions, nails, are better for handling small objects, such as nuts and fruit, and working with tools—something that other mammals rarely do.

Why don't fingernails sweat?

Nails are made of keratin (like hair). This protein is strong and can either be flexible (like hair) or solid (like nails or animal claws and horns). The bits you can see are no longer growing—they are made of dead cells—and so they don't sweat. The growing takes place on the skin underneath the hard nail.

Is it bad to bite your nails?

Chewing on dirty nails can introduce germs into your body, and lead to infections if you damage the skin.

Why do nails grow so fast?

Fingernails protect the sensitive nerve endings of your fingertips. They may be strong, but they are easily chipped, broken, or worn away. They need to grow constantly to perform their task in life. On average, they grow about 3.5 mm (0.14 in) per month. Toenails do the same job, but are subject to less wear and tear, so they grow at a slower rate—around 1.6 mm (0.06 in) per month.

Crunchy!

25

Why do I have to shower?

Have people always washed?

Yes, even in ancient history. So you have no excuse for soap dodging! Ancient Rome's Baths of Caracalla could hold 1,600 bathers at the same time.

Your body has many ways of fighting back against illness and infection. But we can do a lot to help it fight off bacteria and viruses. Sensible cleaning habits, known as hygiene, can remove those harmful germs—which are too small for us to see.

What is an infection?

Micro-organism is the scientific name for the tiny, invisible germs all around us. Some of these bacteria and viruses are safe or even helpful. But harmful micro-organisms can enter the body, where they multiply quickly and cause illnesses. Such an invasion is called an infection.

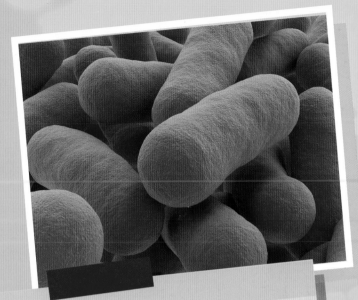

Can doing the laundry fight disease?

Washing can kill disease-carrying fleas and bedbugs living in dirty clothes and blankets.

What if your hands look clean?

It's important to wash your hands regularly, and especially before you eat. Because germs are small enough to be invisible, you might think that your hands are completely clean. But your hands are constantly touching other things—doorknobs, books, or other people's hands—and that contact transmits germs.

How is your body like a building?

Every building needs protection on the outside, and strong supports running through it to stop it from toppling over. Your body is just the same. Without the support provided by your bones, you'd flop over like a rag doll. The framework of bones is called the skeleton.

Are all your bones joined together?

Most of the bones in your skeleton are linked (see page 34) but your hyoid bone, in your throat, is not connected to any other bones.

What does your skeleton protect?

Your body contains many delicate organs such as the heart, lungs, and brain. It hurts even if your your tough outer layers get bumped. Things would be far worse if your skeleton didn't protect your sensitive internal organs.

How have humans changed?

Modern humans have more delicate bones and rounder heads than our ancestors who lived 4 million years ago.

How do our bones tell a story?

Most parts of a body decompose (break down) after a person dies. Bones take much longer to decompose, and can even become fossils, so they can tell us about our ancestors many thousands or even millions of years ago. Scientists can tell how humans have changed and what type of injuries and illnesses ancient humans faced.

How many bones are there in your body?

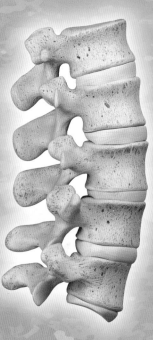

A human adult skeleton contains 206 bones. There are several types of bones. Your fingers, toes, arms, and legs contain long bones. Your wrists and feet have short bones for support and stability. Flat bones, including your hips, ribs, and shoulder blades, are strong for protecting vital organs.

What is your spine made of?

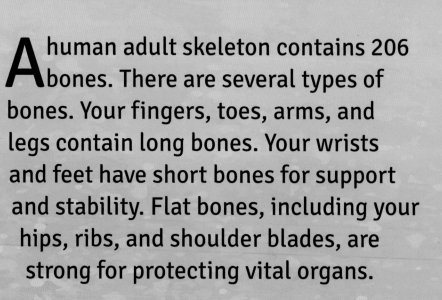

A human spine has 33 disc-shaped backbones, called vertebrae, linked in a long line. They form a tunnel through the middle to protect your spinal cord. Most mammals have seven vertebrae in their neck section, whether they are as tiny as a mouse or as tall as a giraffe!

Can we change our bones?

Eating the right foods helps to make your bones strong and hard (see page 46). Exercise also strengthens bones. Over time, the bones of athletes become tougher and thicker. Bones in the arm a tennis player uses regularly are often larger than in their other arm.

How many bones do we have in our head?

Your brain is protected by eight, flat, bony plates, which form your skull.

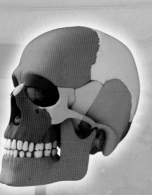

Why don't bones break when you jump?

When you leap and run, your bones don't break. They're tough enough to deal with all your movements. But they aren't solid white stuff all the way through. Bones have a hard outer layer that supports your weight but is light enough to let you move. Inside, though, are living tissues performing many jobs for your whole body.

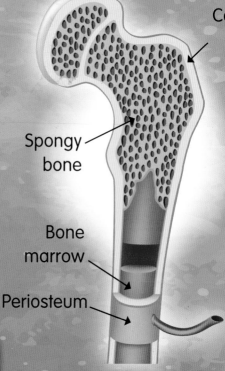

Compact bone

Spongy bone

Bone marrow

Periosteum

What's inside a bone?

The hard white outside of a bone is called compact bone. Nerves and blood vessels of the periosteum, a thin membrane, nourish this outer layer. The layer of spongy bone inside helps keep your bones flexible. The soft marrow, found inside many bones, is like a factory producing blood cells for the whole body.

How do bones help us to hear?

Tiny bones inside your ear carry sound vibrations to your brain, where they are converted into information about what you heard.

Heel bone

Metatarsals (foot bones)

Ligament

Whoo!

What joins bones together?

Bones link to other networks in the body to give it strength and support. Tough tissues called ligaments connect bones to other bones, so that you can move bits of your body. Bones are also connected to muscles, with strong bands of tissue called tendons.

Can people make artificial bones?

Scientists have produced hard bone-like material but are still trying to find ways of linking it to blood vessels.

Can bones bend?

Bones are flexible, so they don't snap in half at the first sign of stress. However, they don't bend very much. Instead, we move our body into different positions using the connections between bones. Your skeleton is helped by joints, muscles, tendons, and ligaments.

I'm so hip!

Do bones scrape together?

A flexible tissue called cartilage covers bones meeting at joints. It reduces friction and lets them move more freely.

Which are your body's strongest ligaments?

The ligaments connecting your hip and leg bones need to support the most weight and also need to be flexible—enough to do splits, for example.

How do bones move?

Your bones meet each other at junctions, called joints. Some joints, like your knees, work like hinges and let bones swing back and forth. Others, like your shoulders, allow even more movement. In each case, tough tissues called ligament attach to both bones and act like pulleys.

What's the difference between a sprain and a strain?

Sometimes one of your joints gets twisted beyond its normal range. This movement can stretch and damage the ligaments, causing a sprain. Strains happen when you overstretch a muscle. They are very common in sports such as basketball. Both sprains and strains can often take longer to heal than a broken bone.

STRE-E-E-TCH!

Do our bones grow bigger?

Yes! They grow bigger when you're young, making you taller and stronger. Sometimes they grow very quickly in "growth spurts." They stop getting bigger when you're in your teens. But bone-building continues all through your life. Your bones are constantly renewing themselves so that they can provide support and produce blood cells.

How big is a growth spurt?

A typical spurt is up to 8 cm (3–4 inches) in just a few months but some people grow up to 30 cm (12 inches) in a year.

Leg bones such as the femur are called "long bones."

How do bones grow larger?

"Long bones" such as those in your arms and legs have growth plates at each end. Inside the plates are columns of cartilage (the same tissue as in your nose). The cartilage multiplies, turning into hard bone and pushing the plates further along. With more hardened material, the bones grow longer.

The femurs grow over 40 cm (15 in) long in most adults.

Do we lose bones as we grow older?

No, but some do fuse together. Babies start with more than 300 hard bits, which are mainly cartilage. By the time you are an adult, these will have joined up to leave you with 206 bones.

What makes bones stop growing?

Bone growth depends on hormones: chemicals that the body produces. You inherit growth information from your parents. This tells your body how much growth hormone to produce. When you reach puberty (becoming physically mature), a different hormone tells growth plates to fuse into hard bone, stopping any more growth.

What happens if you break a bone?

Bones, like other parts of your body, are usually able to recover from serious injury. Within minutes of a break, your body starts to heal. It completes its task in stages, first stopping blood from escaping and finishing with a new length of bone where the break had been.

Ouch!!

Why do you need to have a cast?

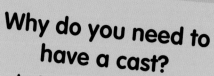

An injured bone can be knocked out of place if it is bumped, so a cast acts as a shock absorber. Sometimes, metal pins are inserted to hold a broken bone in place.

How long does a bone take to mend?

A broken bone can take several months to heal for an adult, but a child's bone often heals within weeks. Bones contain cells that remove and replace old tissue, and other cells to build up new bone. A growing child has more "building" cells than "removing" cells, so the bone can rebuild (or heal) more quickly.

Which is the likeliest bone to break?

The most commonly broken bone for most people is the radius bone in the wrist. Elderly people, though, often break their hips.

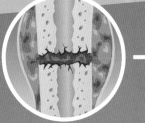 → 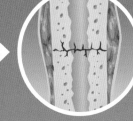 →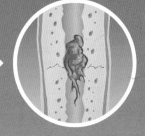

Clot forms   Join toughens   Soft tissue builds   Fracture heals

How does a bone heal itself?

Soon after a break, the bone forms a clot where blood vessels have become exposed. New blood vessels then join this area, turning the clot into tougher connection. Collagen (the main protein in bones) and cartilage build up, and then new cells arrive to turn these soft tissues into hard bone.

Can bones get sick?

Any part of your body can become injured or diseased. If it happens to your bones, your body can lose mobility and support, as well as some of its ability to produce new blood cells. Some conditions arise because of wear and tear, but infections can also develop quickly.

What diseases affect bones?

Much like other parts of the body, bones can become diseased if infections are carried in through blood vessels. Other conditions occur because people inherit them (like having weak or brittle bones) or through constant use. Arthritis often develops because the cartilage between bones becomes thinner, so that bones rub together painfully.

Is arthritis just an old person's disease?

Most people who develop arthritis are in their forties or older, but young people can sometimes be affected. Proper treatment can control it.

Do older people have weaker bones?

Bones are like factories, constantly working. They produce blood cells all the time, but as people get older some of this work slows down. Bone-building cells, which constantly renew bones, often can't keep bones as strong. Bones become less dense—and weaker—as a result.

Do people shrink as they get older?

As people age, gravity takes its toll on the spine. The discs between the vertebrae get squeezed, so people can look a little bit shorter.

How do X-rays show your bones?

Doctors can use special equipment to get clear images of your bones and other parts of your body beneath your skin. X-ray photography is the most common method of checking how your bones are developing—or healing, if they've been injured.

KER-CHINGGG!

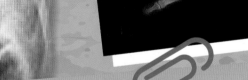

Do X-rays just show bones?
X-ray images give clear pictures of screws and pins in joints—and sometimes even show things that people have swallowed.

Why do bones show up so clearly?

X-rays are waves of light with more energy than the "normal" light we can see. This extra energy allows them to pass through soft tissue such as skin. Harder, denser tissue such as bones stops the waves. An X-ray machine zaps the light through the body and onto special photographic film. The bones show up as white areas where the X-rays could not reach the film.

What else can X-rays show?

A doctor with an X-ray can see if anything is wrong inside a person, but other professionals also use this technology to save lives. If you pass your bags through an X-ray machine at an airport, the staff will be able to see the contents inside. They can check for dangerous or banned items without opening the luggage.

Can bones be fat?

Your bones can't grow fatter, but they do store fat inside. Bones hold emergency supplies of energy, stored as fat in yellow bone marrow. They also store vital minerals that your body needs to function, and the blood cells they produce help you stay healthy and recover from injury.

Bone marrow cell

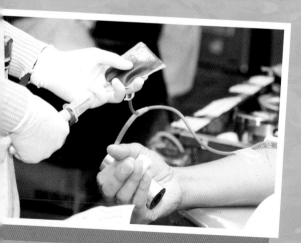

What is a transplant?

In a healthy person, bone marrow produces cells for the whole body. Some health conditions prevent this from happening properly. Healthy cells from one person's marrow can be transplanted into a sick person's body to help their marrow work better. Blood can also be taken from one person and given to another person if they need it.

How active is bone marrow?

Red bone marrow can produce up to 5 billion blood cells each day.

Do young bones work harder?

Nearly all of your bones contain red marrow when you're born and throughout most of your childhood. After that, the number of bones with red marrow declines. That means that adults have fewer blood-cell-producing bones than children. It's why children heal faster—and grow.

When are bones strongest?

Young bones get stronger as part of the growing process, especially if you eat well and exercise. They are strongest in your twenties. After that, bone strength decreases unless you exercise regularly.

How do bones stay strong?

The chemical element calcium is an important ingredient for helping your bones rebuild and stay strong. Some foods, especially dairy products (including ice cream), contain calcium. You also need Vitamin D to help your body extract the calcium from food.

You have two bones in each leg below the knee.

Why is sunshine good for bones?

Some things you eat will give you Vitamin D, but sensible exposure to sunlight is the best way to get a regular dose. Chemicals in your skin can transform the sunshine into a form of Vitamin D. You only need around 20 minutes, then you can nip into the shade again.

Can you eat bones?

You should avoid most bones in your food as they can damage your insides, but soft fish bones like those in tinned salmon are a great source of extra calcium.

Do you keep the same bones all your life?

Your bones are constantly rebuilding themselves—you have a new skeleton about every seven years.

How do helmets protect your skull?

Protective clothing and pads shield people from forces that could injure or break bones. Bike helmets help to protect your skull and your brain. Their hard outer layer spreads the force of an impact from one area. The softer, inner layer absorbs that force so that less of it reaches your head.

MUSCLES AND MOVEMENT

Why do we need muscles?

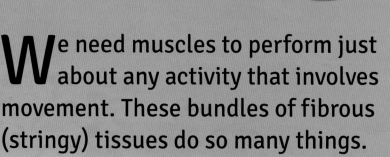

We need muscles to perform just about any activity that involves movement. These bundles of fibrous (stringy) tissues do so many things. They move your bones, open your eyes, and help you chew. Many of them work automatically, pumping your heart, helping you digest food, and making sure you breathe regularly.

Why can you hear your heart?

Each thump of your heartbeat is the sound of a heart muscle forcing a heart valve (part of the heart that controls the flow of blood) shut.

How many muscles make your smile?

People use many combinations of muscles to make a variety of smiles: between ten and 43 muscles for any smile.

Which muscles make you talk?

Your tongue, a collection of muscles, forms many sounds. Even opening and closing your mouth to form other sounds depends on muscles in your face and jaw. And in order to force the air out of your mouth to make a sound, you need to use the diaphragm muscle below your lungs.

How are we moving when we're keeping still?

Imagine that your body is a factory. It may look calm and quiet outside, but inside there is lots going on. Goods are being moved around, doors are opening and closing, and fuel is powering all of the machines. Your muscles keep your body "factory" up and running, even if you're not moving around.

What do muscles look like?

If you looked closely at an elastic band you'd see that it is made up of strands that stretch and then tighten up again. Close up, muscles look a lot like that, but they have special shapes to match their job. All of them respond to signals from your brain, telling them to contract (tighten) or relax.

Do your eyes really have muscles?

Yes! The iris has a muscle that opens and closes the pupil to control incoming light, and there are six muscles around your eye that move your eyeball.

How many muscles are there in your body?

Your body has about 640 muscles. Some people consider some of those to be groups of smaller muscles, so the total could be much higher. Whatever the number, they make up three main groups: skeletal (which move bones), cardiac (in your heart), and smooth (mainly in your digestive system).

How big is your heart?

Lock your hands together with the fingers entwined. That's about the size of your heart.

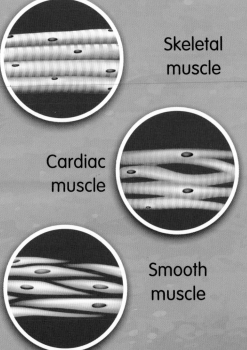

Skeletal muscle

Cardiac muscle

Smooth muscle

What are different muscles like?

Skeletal muscles are made of light and dark bands called fibrils, making them looked striped. They are the only muscles that we control, and most are connected to bones. Cardiac muscles, which pump blood in and out of the heart, are also made up of shaded bands. The smooth muscles on the walls of many internal organs get their name because they lack stripes.

How do muscles help us move?

Skeletal muscles help you move around. They are connected to bones with tough tissues called tendons and work by pulling rather than pushing. As a muscle contracts, it pulls a tendon connected to a bone. That pulls the bone with it. You're in control of these muscles, which tighten or relax as you instruct them.

How many muscles does it take to walk?

The simple act of taking a step involves several movements. You need to lift one leg off the floor, move it forward, place it back down, and keep your balance at the same time. This uses muscles in your hips, bottom, thighs, lower leg, feet, toes, and also your arms, waist, tummy, and back. At a rough count, it's around 200 muscles!

Bulging biceps!

Do different people have different muscles?

We all have the same number of muscles, but their shape and size differ. That gives some people a head start in certain activities, such as long distance running or swimming.

Why do muscles work in pairs?

Muscles often pair up on each side of a bone or joint. When you bend your arm, you're tightening the biceps muscle on one side of your upper arm. At the same time, you're relaxing the triceps muscle underneath. To straighten out again you just do the opposite with the pair.

Which is your largest muscle?

The largest muscles in your body are the gluteus maximus muscles in your bottom. They move your back and your largest bone, the femur (thigh bone).

CRE-E-E-A-K!!

53

Can muscles really remember?

It's true that muscles can seem to remember a series of movements in the right order. It's called muscle memory. But in reality, it's your brain that's calling the shots. Like a computer with a set of stored commands, your brain stores a series of signals that it sends out to muscles when certain actions are needed.

Does practice always make perfect?

Unfortunately, muscle memory doesn't necessarily make you do things better. It can also stop you from improving, if you keep making the same mistakes.

Why do we need muscle memory?

Imagine having to think about every movement of your arm whenever you served a tennis ball, or every single twist of your fingers when you tie your shoes. Luckily your muscles can be trained to do repeated actions the same way again and again.

Can it help you play the piano?

Yes, as long as you learn the correct notes. Age is no barrier to muscle memory—Jacob Velazquez from Florida could play entire works by Beethoven when he was five.

Can artificial muscles develop a memory?

Many artificial limbs combine smooth movement with comfort, but until recently, the "muscles" in these limbs couldn't perform repeated actions as quickly as human muscles. Scientists have now developed ways of chemically recording the movements of artificial limbs so that they can perform patterns of movement quickly, just like human muscles.

Can muscles work by themselves?

Your body never shuts off. It's working 24/7, even if you're asleep. Muscles provide the movement and activity to keep things running. Involuntary, or smooth, muscles line the walls of organs and blood vessels. Their contractions help move blood, food, and other substances through the body.

How does your heart keep in rhythm?

The outer walls of your heart contain a group of muscle cells which produce a small electrical current. These electrical pulses make your heart beat at a safe, steady pace.

Can your muscles turn you into a caveman?

When you're suddenly scared, your brain sends a signal to glands that produce a chemical called epinephrine (or adrenalin). Your heart rate speeds up and blood rushes to your muscles, ready for you to fight anything dangerous - or run away from it, just as early humans would once have done when under attack.

Aarrghh!

Can heart muscles mix up signals?

Yes, they can. Some people can have an irregular heartbeat treated with a device called a pacemaker, which sends out regular pulses to the cardiac muscles.

Why do we breathe faster sometimes?

Your diaphragm muscle controls your breathing. The speed it works at depends on how much carbon dioxide (a waste product) is in your blood. If there's a lot, like when you exercise, then you breathe fast. If levels are low, like when you're asleep, then your brain tells your diaphragm to make you breathe more slowly. It's automatic.

How do muscles build up?

If you and a weightlifter stood next to each other and flexed your muscles, the weightlifter's muscles would look much bigger than yours. Weightlifters build up their muscles by lifting heavy loads. But it's more important that you keep your muscles strong with regular exercise than focus on bodybuilding!

Do all exercises build up muscles?

Different forms of exercise help keep muscles strong, but some weightlifting causes tiny rips in the muscles. Those muscles get a little bigger (or bulk up) as they heal.

How heavy are weightlifters' weights?

In deadlifting competitions, weightlifters regularly lift 500 kg (1,100 lb) weights up to thigh level. That's about the weight of an adult zebra!

Can you lengthen your muscles?

It's impossible to lengthen your muscles, because they are attached to tendons and bones at each end. They grow when you're young but stop when you reach adult height. Imagine a road linking two cities. You couldn't lengthen that road, but you could widen it. Bulking out muscles widens them.

What are your core muscles?

It's not only your arms and legs that use muscles. Your central body has muscles that are extremely important for all-round movement. The muscles in your stomach (your "abs" or "six-pack") and lower back keep you strong and help you sit up straighter, walk better, and feel good if they are toned.

What is a muscle cramp?

Chemicals are exchanged each time muscles contract and relax. The tissues in a resting muscle are long and stretched. When the tissues tighten and the muscle contracts, calcium rushes in and sodium (salt) goes out. Normally the muscle relaxes again quickly, but sometimes it stays tightly and painfully constricted. That's muscle cramp.

What causes a stitch in your side?

The sharp pain in your side when you exercise is thought to be a cramp in the diaphragm. Stretch to the opposite side from the stitch to relieve it.

Does exercise after eating cause cramps?

Probably not, but you are likely to feel sick or sluggish if you exercise too soon after eating. During exercise, your blood flow is diverted to your muscles from your digestive system. This can make it harder to deal with large amounts of food.

Do muscles ever move by mistake?

Involuntary muscle movements (called tics or twitches) are usually temporary and caused when nerve endings accidentally fire a signal to a muscle.

Glug glug!!

Are cramps bad for you?

Most cramps are harmless results of exercising too much or too fast, or not drinking enough water beforehand. That makes it harder for muscles to receive and get rid of nutrients or waste. However, very severe, prolonged, or frequent cramps could be signs of wider medical problems.

Do muscles need special fuel?

Muscles get most of their energy from glucose, a type of sugar that is found in many foods. They use oxygen contained in the blood to convert the glucose into energy. This is a chemical reaction, and it also releases water and carbon dioxide. The energy can be used straight away or stored as fuel for later.

Why do tennis players eat bananas?

Bananas contain lots of carbohydrates (which release glucose) as well as potassium, which helps prevent cramps.

ACE!

Does a balanced diet help muscles?

A balanced diet usually refers to eating a sensible mixture of foods providing protein, fat, and carbohydrates. That balance helps most of your body's systems, and is especially good for muscles. Carbohydrates such as potatoes, pasta, and grains provide energy. Fat stores some of that energy, and protein is the "building block" of muscles.

Is losing weight bad for your muscles?

Yes, because if people try to lose weight too fast, their bodies might use muscles, rather than fat, as a source of energy.

Are energy drinks helpful?

Energy drinks promise to promote strength and alertness, but often rely on lots of sugar (to provide glucose) and caffeine (the drug in coffee that keeps people awake). You shouldn't have too much of either of these. Instead, eat a banana for energy, drink water to stop dehydration, and have a glass of chocolate milk after you've done a sport; it provides a great mix of nutrients for your muscles. Yummy!

Why does exercise "burn" sometimes?

Have you heard people talk about "feeling the burn" when their muscles are working hard? That's because oxygen in your blood helps your muscles use glucose to produce energy. If you're exercising really hard, then the muscles use up all the oxygen in the blood nearby. The muscles now start to turn sugar into oxygen. Lactic acid is left behind, giving your muscles a burning feeling.

Does exercise make you happy?

Scientists have found that muscles that work hard produce chemicals called endorphins, which send "I feel happy" signals to the brain.

Can we exercise too much?

Feeling the burn is a sign that your muscles have been working hard. That can be a good thing, but it's also one of the signals that things have gone too far and that you need rest. If too much lactic acid is left behind, then your muscles can be damaged.

How much exercise do you need?

Young people should try to do one hour every day. It doesn't matter what form the exercise takes, as long as it makes you breathe faster and sweat a little. It can be dancing, swimming, skateboarding, playing ball games, climbing trees, martial arts, riding your bike, or running around the block with your dog.

Do older people need to exercise?

Some muscle turns to fat as people get older, so it's important to exercise regularly to keep those muscle levels maintained.

How do muscles keep us warm?

As well as "feeling the burn" and "burning calories," muscles really can produce heat, and help you to keep warm when the outside temperature starts to fall. Calories measure a form of heat linked to energy. That energy provides fuel for your muscles to act like a central heating system.

What happens when we shiver?

Your body can sense when cold is a threat. The brain sends signals to muscles on your skin, making them contract and relax very quickly. As they do so, they release heat.

Can muscles shrink?

If muscles aren't used enough, they become small and weak. Astronauts use less muscle in space because they aren't working against gravity the whole time. To make up for this they have to exercise every day. On the International Space Station, astronauts spend over two hours per day working out.

Phew!

What causes goose bumps?

Muscles cause tiny hairs on your body to stand up, pulling skin up in bumps. The standing hairs trap warm air to act as a blanket against the cold. The scientific name is horripilation!

Why do athletes warm up before performing?

Warming up is a slow-motion way to prepare your muscles for activity. It helps loosen the muscles, making exercise easier, and it increases your heart and breathing rates to send more blood and oxygen to muscles. Plus, it really does warm up muscles, and warmer muscles can get oxygen from the blood faster.

What is a human organ?

Doctors define organs as collections of tissue formed in a special way to perform particular jobs. There are lots of bodily tasks to be done, and your organs help you do them. Different organs make sense of the world around you, turn food into fuel, send nutrients to where they're needed, and get rid of things that are unhealthy.

Is your eye an organ?

Yes! It is an organ that reacts to light to allow you to see. It is less developed in babies; they only see black and white to begin with.

WOW!!

Do organs work on their own?

Your body is like a football team that has players with different roles who come together to operate as a team. Your kidneys filter waste and turn it into pee, but form part of a larger system called the urinary system. The heart is at the "heart" of the circulatory system. The liver, pancreas, and spleen are part of the digestive system.

How many organs do we have?

Different people count in different ways. We have five vital organs: the brain, lungs, heart, liver, and kidneys, and around 70 others.

Are we born with all our organs?

Our organs form in the months before we are born, so from day one we have a complete set. Some of them, such as the heart, lungs, and liver, have already been working hard. Others, such as the reproductive organs, develop more fully when we are older.

Why does your brain take control?

Keep thinking of your body as being like a team. To be effective, the players (human organs) need to work together. They follow the orders of the coach who has an overview of everything. Your brain is like a coach, constantly observing what's happening and sending out orders to the rest of the body.

Some images, known as optical illusions, can trick the brain.

Does the brain ever get mixed up?

Sometimes your brain receives confusing information and processes it in the best way it can. In an optical illusion like this one, too many bright patterns mean the brain can't process the image. It appears to be spinning on the page.

How does your brain control things?

Your brain can tell which area of your body needs a boost and calls on other areas to help out. If you're exercising really hard, for example, you need more oxygen by your leg muscles. Your brain gets your lungs and heart to work that much harder.

Is there such a thing as "brain food?"

Certain foods are good for your brain. Fish, nuts, broccoli, avocado, and—wait for it—small amounts of dark chocolate can improve memory, learning, and concentration skills.

What can we train our brain to do?

We train our brain when we learn new skills and actions: reading, playing the guitar, or skiing. The brain stores the instructions for later use. These are called conscious activities because we control them. At the same time, the brain does many important jobs automatically. Luckily, we can't un-train our brain to signal how to breathe or digest food.

How much blood does your heart pump?

An adult body has at least 4 l (1 gallon) of blood, which carries oxygen and essential chemicals to every part of the body so that muscles and organs work properly. The blood completes the return journey from those parts, carrying waste. In order to move this amount of blood all the time, you need a strong, reliable pump—your heart.

How much blood is that in a lifetime?

Your heart is made up of two pumps, with extra-strong muscles squeezing them in a rhythm. Your heartbeat—the number of squeezes—is about 90 per minute. With 2.5 billion beats in a typical lifetime, that's the same as your heart moving enough blood to fill 100 Olympic swimming pools.

Rusty!!!

Why does blood look red?

The blood moving around your body contains varying amounts of oxygen. This reacts with an iron-rich protein in your red blood cells, turning it red—just as iron turns rusty red when it meets oxygen in the air. Blood with lots of oxygen is bright red, and gets darker as it releases the oxygen around the body. Some creatures, such as spiders and lobsters, have copper instead of iron in their blood, making it blue.

How far does blood travel?

The human body contains over 96,000 km (60,000 miles) of blood vessels. Blood cells travel along these highways and byways many times every day!

I'm feeling a bit blue...

Why do veins look blue?

On pale-skinned people, the veins close to the surface look blue, not red. They still contain red blood, but they appear blue because of the way light travels through the skin.

Why is it hard to hold your breath?

It starts to hurt if you try to hold your breath for too long. That's your brain telling you to let your lungs do their work. It's their job to get the oxygen from each breath in, and get rid of carbon dioxide and other wastes when you exhale. You need your lungs to provide the breath for moving, speaking, singing, and laughing.

Hmphhh...

How many breaths do you take in a day?
In a typical day, you will breathe in (and out again!) more than 20,000 times.

Do your lungs have muscles?

Your lungs can't breathe without help. And that help comes from a big muscle beneath them, called the diaphragm. When it tightens, air rushes in to your chest (and lungs). Relaxing it reduces the space in your chest, forcing you to breathe out.

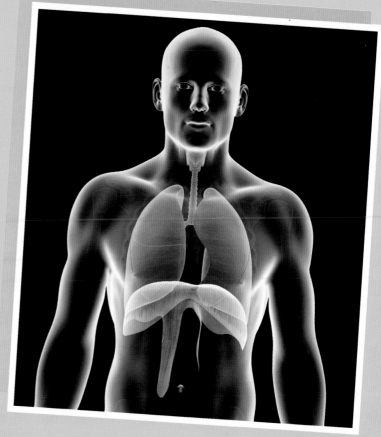

How long can some people hold their breath?

Some deep-sea divers can hold their breath for more than 20 minutes, but most people can manage only a minute.

What's happening when we're out of breath?

Being out of breath is sometimes the sign of an illness, but usually it's because you've been exercising hard. That extra work for your muscles calls for increased oxygen, and sometimes your breathing can't keep pace. You need to stop and steady your breathing until you can continue with your exercise.

What happens to the food you swallow?

Burp!

You know that you need to eat food to provide your body with fuel and nutrients. But solid food—and also what you drink—isn't ready to help you right away. It needs to pass through your body and be digested. The digestive system is a series of long, twisting tubes that link your mouth and your stomach, and lead out through your anus (bottom) at the end.

Why do we burp?

We can easily swallow air along with our food, especially if we eat fast. That air escapes back the way it came in the form of a burp.

Why do we chew food?

Special chemicals called enzymes, contained in your saliva, start to break down what you've eaten. This sets off the process called digestion, or getting useful nutrients from what you eat. Chewing your food makes it easier for the enzymes to begin digesting it. Chewed food also travels more easily down to your stomach.

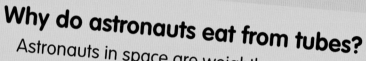

Why do astronauts eat from tubes?

Astronauts in space are weightless, so that everything, including food, floats. Squeezing food from tubes is the best way to stop it from floating away.

Can you digest food if you're upside-down?

Cartoons sometimes show food falling down a chute into the stomach. In reality, the food is squeezed from your mouth to your stomach. The tube that links them is surrounded by rings of muscles. They take it in turns to push the food along. And they work the same way whether you are upside down or the right way up!

How big is your stomach?

Well, it depends on your body size! The organ that is called the stomach is the size of a fist, but it doesn't take up the whole of your "tummy" space. The other parts of your digestive system sit in that space, too. The first stop is the stomach, then food moves on through the intestines.

Do you get a new stomach every few days?

In a way, you really do. The stomach has four layers, and the inner layer comes in contact with strong acids that break down food. That layer is constantly replaced, to protect the other layers (which include strong muscles) from those powerful acids.

Why does your tummy rumble sometimes?

Stomach muscles constantly squeeze food to break it up. Sometimes gases and air are squeezed out of the food... and rumble inside.

How much can your stomach stretch?

Your stomach is shaped like a letter J and has three main jobs: storing food, turning the food into more of a liquid, and sending it on to the small intestine. It needs to be stretchy for that first job, and your stomach can extend to 20 times its resting size after a big meal.

How long does food stay in your stomach?

It takes the stomach about three to four hours to break solid food down into a liquidy mush called chyme. The chyme is then sent on to the intestines.

79

Do other organs deal with your food?

Many of your body's organs have more than one job to do. They need to help extract useful nutrients from your food while also producing important substances of their own. Some lesser-known organs, such as the pancreas and gall bladder, help the "stars" such as the stomach, liver, and intestines do their job.

Gall bladder

Pancreas

Yum!

What do we mean by rich food?

Rich food isn't food for rich people. It is food high in fats, such as butter and cream, that takes longer to digest.

Does our body need sugar?

Too much sugar damages blood vessels but too little robs muscles and organs of fuel. Your pancreas monitors sugar levels in your body. It produces a chemical called insulin to deal with excess sugar and another called glucagon to tell your liver to produce more sugar if levels are low. Diabetes is a disorder where the pancreas cannot process sugar properly.

Testing sugar levels is easy to do.

Why is human waste brown?

The liver produces a chemical called bile that helps digest fats. Extra bile is stored in an organ called the gall bladder. When bile reacts with bacteria in your guts, it turns the waste brown.

Why do we throw up?

Nausea—the sick feeling before you throw up—is a signal that your body needs to get rid of something harmful. Throwing up isn't nice, but you often feel better afterward, proving that it was necessary. Feeling sick is your body's way of giving you a message, just like an ache or pain stops you from using tired or damaged muscles.

Which is your busiest organ?

Your liver performs hundreds of jobs to keep your body working. You absolutely could not live without it—and it is so special that part of a liver can regrow into a whole one. The liver processes your food, stores the energy, gets rid of waste, and cleans your blood, as well as hundreds of other important tasks.

How are liver transplants special?

If you transplant part of a liver, it will grow to normal size in the sick person, and the bit left behind also grows back in the healthy person.

We're digesting!

How big is the liver?

It is the largest internal organ in the body, weighing about 1.4 kg (3 lb). It grows as you do, reaching full size by about age 15: around 15 cm (6 in) across. With more than 500 tasks to perform, from digesting food and breaking down toxins, to helping the blood clot, it's not surprising that the liver is so big.

What poisons does your liver deal with?

External poisons, such as drugs and alcohol, and ammonia, which is created internally by the body's everyday chemical reactions.

What is the liver's most important job?

If you asked ten specialist doctors, you might get ten different answers, because the liver does so much. But the really vital job—sometimes needed to save your life—is to clean the poisons in your system. That's the liver's "emergency department" role, although the other 499 (or more) jobs are important.

How are kidneys like filters?

Your two fist-sized kidneys, located near the middle of your back, filter your blood to remove waste material and excess water. About 200 l (50 gallons) of blood passes through them each day. The blood comes out cleaner and the waste and water gets sent off as urine.

Why is urine sometimes paler?

Urine contains different wastes along with water. Drinking lots of water reduces the concentration of wastes, making urine more watery, and clearer.

What if your kidneys don't work?

You could get by with one kidney, if the other became damaged. But losing a second kidney would cause serious problems because of the build-up of waste in your blood. Dialysis machines can take the place of kidneys, filtering blood and returning it to the patient's body.

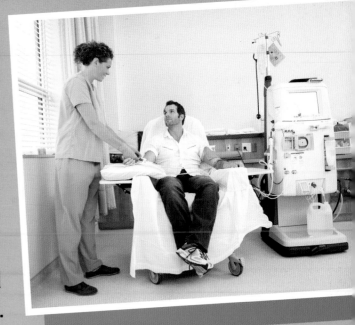

How do you know when you need to pee?

Urine gathers in an organ called the bladder. When it gets full, the bladder sends a message to your brain that it is emptying-out time!

Why are we so full of waste?

Your blood delivers nutrients around your body. Sometimes it brings stuff you already have enough of. Other stuff is broken down by chemical reactions in your cells, which can produce waste products—a bit like a car's exhaust. Water leaves your body as sweat, in your breath, and also in your poop, but the majority of it goes into your urine.

Do some organs just do nothing?

It might seem strange to think that your body carries around excess baggage that serves no purpose. But some parts of your body do seem to be souvenirs of a time when your ancestors—long ago—needed them to survive in very different conditions. Over time these body parts get smaller, but some never go away.

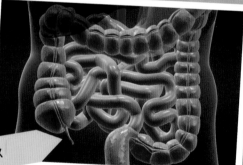

Appendix

What is your appendix for?

The appendix is a small tube attached to your large intestine. That's where your body digests food, except the human appendix doesn't seem to digest anything. Many scientists believe that it once helped human ancestors—like today's apes—to digest twigs and leaves.

Do your ears have muscles?

Your ears do have muscles to move them as monkeys do, except most people (unless they can "wiggle their ears") can't use those muscles.

Do you really have a tail?

If you look behind any of your friends, you won't see any tail. But every human does have a tail bone, called the coccyx, at the base of the back. It's all that's left of a tail that our ancestors had millions of years ago—just as monkeys still have.

Do people have too many teeth?

The four "wisdom teeth" (molars) which develop when you're about 20, were most likely used by our ancestors to grind plants.

5

How many cells are in your body?

Humans, like other living things, are made up of collections of cells. They are the building blocks of your body, able to grow and reproduce. These cells group together to become the systems that oversee all the work for the body to stay healthy. It's hard to judge how many there are, but scientists' recent estimates come in at around 37 trillion!

How many red blood cells do we have?

There are around five million red cells in just a single drop of human blood. Men usually have more than women.

What do cells do?

They carry out special jobs like providing energy, fighting attackers, carrying away waste, and much more. Groups of similar cells teaming up are called tissue. Lots of tissue working together is known as an organ and the biggest collection of cells—working all over your body in different networks—becomes known as a system.

Can you see cells with your naked eye?

You need a microscope to see individual cells, but you can see collections of cells (tissues and organs) easily.

Wheeee!

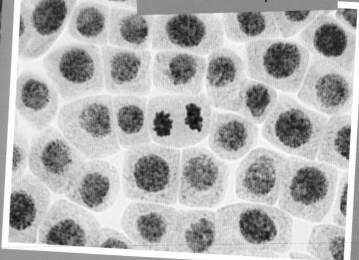

Human tissue cells seen under a microscope.

Why are cells different shapes?

To help them perform different tasks. Red blood cells, for example, are shaped like donuts as it's the best way to float in your blood where they carry oxygen. Nerve cells have long sections that look like tiny wires—ideal for carrying electrical signals to your brain and other parts of your body.

How many systems does the body have?

Hey, guess what? Different experts say different numbers. The science of the body isn't that straightforward! However, there are at least ten systems carrying out the jobs in your body that make you work so well. Here are some of them.

CIRCULATORY SYSTEM
Carries blood around your body.

NERVOUS SYSTEM
Carries messages and sends signals.

SKELETAL SYSTEM
Supports, protects, and moves you around.

Is your skin an organ or a system?

The answer is... both! It's the body's largest organ but the way that it combines fighting disease, storing fat, and getting rid of waste makes it a system as well.

Do systems work in isolation?

No—often two or more systems work together to get a job done. Your muscles, for example, need oxygen and nutrients delivered. The respiratory system keeps you supplied with oxygen, and the circulatory system delivers that oxygen to every part of your body. Similar pairings help you digest food, get rid of waste, and combat infection.

Does resting help your body's systems?
Regular rest, or taking time off after exercise, helps your systems maintain their strength.

RESPIRATORY SYSTEM
Brings in air and removes carbon dioxide.

MUSCULAR SYSTEM
Helps you move, breathe, and function.

DIGESTIVE SYSTEM
Breaks down food and removes waste.

How did you start out?

The tiniest amount of material from your mother and father combined to set things under way to produce something special—you. Contained inside that material was all the information your body would need to become a human being.

What are multiple births?

A fertilized egg sometimes divides, producing identical twins or even triplets. Non-identical twins develop when sperm cells reach two separate egg cells.

I'm winning!

Do we really start out as two cells?

A sperm cell from your father combined with—or fertilized—an egg cell inside your mother. The sperm had competition from hundreds of millions of other sperm cells, each trying to reach the single egg cell. Women usually produce just one egg cell each month.

How much do babies weigh?

Most babies weigh between 2.7 and 4.1 kg (6–9 lb) but record-breaking babies can weigh over 10 kg (22 lb)!

How long do we live inside our mother?

The period from that first meeting of sperm and egg cells all the way to the birth of a baby is called gestation. It normally takes about 40 weeks. During that time we develop and grow so that we're able to eat and breathe as soon as we are born.

How does blood travel?

Your blood travels along a network of large and small channels called blood vessels. It goes out from the heart and lungs along arteries and returns along veins to be refreshed. This out-and-back movement is called circulating, so your blood is part of your circulatory system.

How fast does blood travel?

It takes just about a minute for blood to make the journey from your heart, around your body, and back to your heart again.

What exactly is blood?

Your blood is a combination of red cells (to carry oxygen), white cells (to fight infection), platelets (to stop bleeding), and a yellowish liquid called plasma. In addition to feeding and protecting your body, blood can cool you down by sending heat to your skin when you're too warm inside. That's why many people look red-faced when they're hot.

Red blood cell

Platelet

White blood cell

Plasma

What causes a bruise?

A bump to your body can cause tiny blood vessels to break. Blood leaks out of the broken vessels and fills part of the area. Damaged blood cells flow toward the surface of the skin, showing up as a bruise around the injured area.

What are the smallest blood vessels?

The tiniest blood vessels, where blood is passed to surrounding tissue, are called capillaries: some are only one cell wide.

How does your body carry messages?

Your body needs a network to send messages back and forth—calling for more blood or for help to fight infection, or just to pass on how good a pizza smells. The nervous system does that job, relaying signals up to the brain and out to everywhere in your body.

What is a reflex?

A reflex is an instant and automatic reaction that the body uses to protect itself—like blinking in the light or pulling your hand away from a flame.

How does your brain make sense of information?

The central nervous system consists of the brain and the spinal cord (inside the backbone). Incoming information is processed in special areas concentrating on sound, sight, movement, and so on. Sensory nerves send impulses to the brain and motor nerves send signals out.

What happens when we blush?

Your body reacts to an awkward event by releasing adrenaline. This causes more blood to flow, especially to your face (where there are many blood vessels).

Are your nerves full of electricity?

The nervous system links billions of nerve cells, or neurons, in a series of paths leading to and from your brain. The signals that travel along this network are called impulses. The impulses combine electricity and chemistry to jump from one neuron to the next along the way. The gap between neurons is called a synapse.

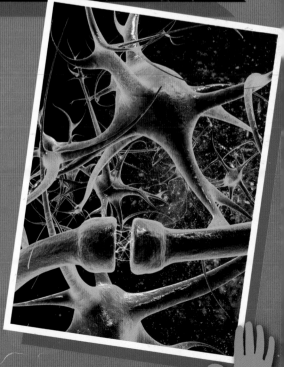

Do all living things breathe?

Animals and plants both need certain gases to live, and must get rid of other harmful gases. Even bacteria use respiration to stay alive. Plants must take in carbon dioxide and "breathe out" oxygen. We do the opposite—inhaling to get oxygen and exhaling to get rid of carbon dioxide and other wastes.

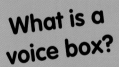

What is a voice box?

It's the scientific term for the larynx, which has tissue folds (vocal cords) that vibrate to make sounds when air passes through.

How much oxygen is in the air?

About one fifth of the air we breathe is oxygen. The rest of it is mostly nitrogen, with tiny amounts of other gases. Our body doesn't extract all of that oxygen: the air we exhale still has around one sixth oxygen, plus the carbon dioxide produced as waste.

Does exercise help your lungs?

Your muscles work better if you exercise regularly. Gradually, they need less oxygen and produce less carbon dioxide—so exercise gives your lungs a helping hand.

How do muscles get oxygen?

Oxygen is transported through your circulatory system in red blood cells. Muscles need oxygen just as a fire needs air: to burn things. Your muscles use oxygen to burn sugars and fats in order to release energy through chemical reactions.

How does your body fight disease?

Your immune system is able to call on most other systems to do something very important—keep you healthy by defending against viruses, bacteria, and parasites. It can identify a problem, find the right weapons for a battle, and make sure that you're prepared next time you face that threat.

AAAHH!

STREPTOCOCCUS
These beastly bacteria can cause sore throats.

Are bacteria always bad?

No. More than 500 different types of bacteria help your body digest food, get rid of waste… and kill bad bacteria.

What is the lymphatic system?

Your body has a network of channels that transport lymph, a clear liquid containing proteins and white blood cells to fight disease. The lymph also transports wastes away, filtering them out at special junctions called lymph nodes. Those nodes have extra supplies of disease-fighting white blood cells and proteins.

Should you really "starve a fever?"

Yes. If you eat, kick-starting your digestive system into action, it will give your body extra work when it really needs to focus on other tasks.

Can a fever be good for you?

Yes. Not only does it act as an external signal that you are sick, it is also your body's way of fighting germs. A section of your brain turns up the temperature in your body to make it too hot for germs to take hold.

What happens to the food we eat?

You might want to eat ice cream and chocolates all day, but your body needs different types of fuel to operate as it should. It relies on the digestive system to turn roast beef, broccoli, spaghetti, and cupcakes—in other words, food—into fuel for your body.

When do you begin to digest food?

Even before you take a bite! When you see food and your mouth waters, you're preparing saliva to start digesting.

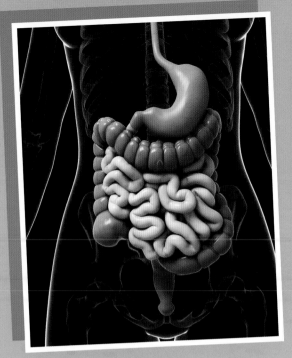

Why are your intestines so long?

Your small intestine (which is longer but skinnier than your large intestine) absorbs nutrients from food as it passes along the way. Its length—about 6 m (20 ft) if uncoiled—gives it lots of surface area to capture food. That surface area is increased further with lots of finger-like shapes called villi.

How long does it take to digest a big meal?

From the time you finish your meal until the last bit of goodness has been extracted can take up to eight hours. Food passes from the stomach to the small intestine and then into the large intestine. What's left is sent off as waste.

Why doesn't your stomach digest itself?

Strong acid in your stomach breaks down food, but your stomach lining has a layer of slimy mucus to protect it from the acid.

What do hormones do?

They are chemical messengers, transporting information between your cells. Hormones are produced in your body's glands and keep control of your growth, moods, metabolism (obtaining fuel from food), and reproduction. Together, they make up the endocrine system.

Hypothalamus

Pituitary gland

Do men and women have the same glands?

Mostly, but they do have different reproductive glands—the ovaries and testes—that allow people to have babies.

How many glands do we have?

The human body has eight major glands, all controlled by stimulation from the nervous system. Your brain is the home of two very important ones: the pituitary and the hypothalamus. The former is the "master" gland that controls other glands in the body, and produces the growth hormones that make you taller and stronger. The hypothalamus regulates body temperature, hunger and thirst, and your moods.

Do all glands make hormones?

No. Some make substances to be released from your body, such as tears, sweat, spit, and a woman's milk for her baby.

YAWN...

Can glands send you to sleep?

They can and they do! Your pineal gland is the shape of a pinecone and is also located in your brain. It is sensitive to changes in the light and produces a hormone called melatonin as the light fades. This hormone makes you feel sleepy, to control your natural sleep-wake patterns.

MEOYAWN...

Why are people different heights?

Diet sometimes plays a part in how fast we grow, and of course, people might wear high heels, but they can't really change how tall they'll eventually become. Like much of what makes you you, this information was determined in your cells even before you were born. You can probably thank – or blame – your parents.

What's the tallest a person can grow?

Anything over 1.8 m (6 ft) is above average, although it's not uncommon for men to grow up to 2.1 m (7 ft). One of the tallest men ever, Robert Wadlow, wore adult clothes when he was five years old, and grew to be 2.72 m (8 ft 11 in)!

Why are men generally taller than women?

Scientists have many different answers to why men are taller—ranging from the needs of our ancient ancestors (now part of our genes) to just the importance of having men and women look different. The mechanics are easier to explain: girls mature earlier and stop growing, while boys have an extra two or three years to grow.

What turns hair silver?

Over time, hair cells lose the pigment (like a dye) that made hair red or black... and the transparent hair looks silver or white.

Why do some people have red hair?

Our cells contain complicated sets of information, like computer programs. These are called genes, and they have instructions (passed on from our parents) about our eyes, height, intelligence... and whether our hair will be red or brown or fair or black.

How busy is your brain?

Think of everything that's going on around you right now. Even while you're concentrating on thinking about it, thousands of other things are happening, both around you and inside your body. Luckily your brain can make sense of it all, and avoid total confusion.

Does your brain need exercise?

Yes! Doctors recommend reading, playing musical instruments, and doing puzzles as ways of keeping the brain "fit" well into old age.

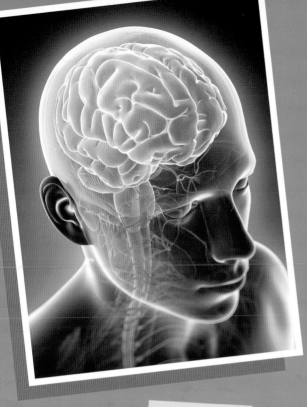

Does your brain work like a computer?

In many ways your brain is like a computer, constantly analyzing data and acting on that stimulation. But even the most advanced computer can't match the brain in quickly sending information back along its own system. The most powerful computer is still 30 times slower than your brain!

How big is the human brain?

An adult brain weighs around 1.5 kg (3.3 lb)—about the same as a medium oven-ready chicken. It measures about 15 cm (6 in) long.

No monkey business!

Do we notice everything around us?

We often focus on one thing and ignore other activities. It's called selective attention. In one experiment, scientists ask viewers to count how often a group of basketball players pass the ball in a short video clip. People concentrate on counting, but often miss the man in a gorilla costume that walks through the group of players!

Why do you need your eyes?

Sight is one of the most important human senses, and saying "I see" in many languages means "I understand." Your eyes do an excellent job of observing what's happening around you and sending that information to your brain. Sight is so important that around half of your brain is involved in seeing. But sometimes even these precision tools need adjusting.

What happens when we see double?

If your eyes aren't looking in exactly the same direction, your brain can't form a single, 3-D image so you see two images.

Why do we have two eyes?

Light and images pass through your eye and reach the retina, where they're turned into electrical signals and sent off to the brain. One eye could do this job well, but it wouldn't be able to help you judge depth, or distance. The brain judges the slightly different images from the two eyes and works out how far away objects are.

Are both your eyes always the same?

Not always. Some children develop a "lazy eye" which sees less clearly than the other eye.

How do glasses help people see?

Images pass through lenses (curved, clear bits of tissue) on your eye on their way to the retina. Sometimes the lenses lose their shape and no longer send clear images—like an out-of-focus photograph. Glasses have special lenses to correct these problems.

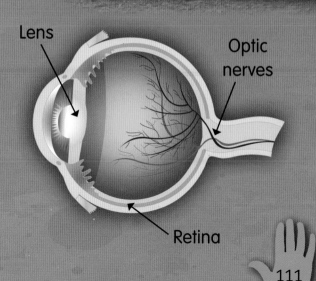

Lens

Optic nerves

Retina

How do you hear sounds?

Sounds are made by vibrations that create waves which pass through the air and are captured by our ears. It's the ears' job to turn those air vibrations into electrical signals that get sent to the brain. Like a radio receiving its signals, the brain transforms those into the sounds we hear.

Can loud noises hurt you?

Very loud noises can kill cells in the inner ear, so over time, if enough of these cells die, a person can suffer from hearing loss.

Do your ears make you seasick?

The inner ear has two jobs. One is to translate vibrations into electrical sound signals. The other is to help your sense of balance. Your brain analyzes fluid inside your inner ear to keep you upright and balanced. You can get seasick if the information from this fluid level doesn't match the information sent from your eyes.

It's all about the balance...

Is it possible to have complete silence?

Not really... even inside soundproof containers, people still hear the hums, thumps, and buzzes of their own heart and nerves.

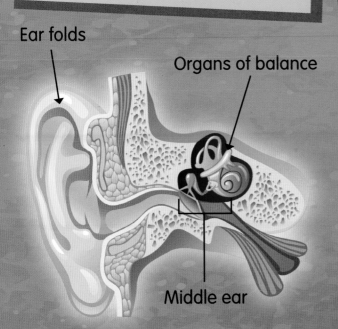

Ear folds

Organs of balance

Middle ear

Why do ears have those folds of skin?

Those folds act like a funnel, trapping sound waves and sending them into your ear even more strongly. The waves cause tiny bones in your middle ear to vibrate. And those vibrations cause even tinier cells in your inner ear to send electrical signals to the brain, which registers them as sounds.

What can your skin feel?

Ouch!

In case you've forgotten, your skin is your body's largest organ. It has many jobs to do, apart from protecting what's inside it. One of the most important is to send signals from its receptors—which are sensitive to heat, cold, and pressure—to the brain. It's your sense of touch.

Why do I "burn" my tongue?

Your tongue is sensitive to pain and pressure, but it is not so sensitive to heat. Sometimes, we drink things that are too hot, but we don't realize until our tongue is already "burned."

Why are some parts of your body more sensitive?

The skin is packed with nerve endings, known as sensors, which pick up signals and send them on to the brain. Specialized sensors detect pressure, heat, cold, pain, and itches. Some parts of your body, such as your fingertips and face, are loaded with sensors. Others, such as your back and belly, have fewer sensors, and so are less sensitive.

How do people read by touch?

Many blind people can use their fingers to follow patterns of raised dots on a page, using the Braille writing system.

What happens when we're tickled?

The nerve signals from a light touch pass near the part of the brain that detects pleasure. That's why we usually laugh when we're tickled. But the brain also filters out unimportant information. So if you try to tickle yourself, your brain isn't fooled and it ignores the urge to laugh.

Can you really taste with your nose?

Does your mouth water when you smell a lasagna cooking in the oven? And do you find that you can't taste food when your head is blocked up with a cold? These are examples of how your nose and mouth act as a team to guide your sense of taste.

Do women have a better sense of smell than men?

Tests suggest that women do, but the reason might be linked to practice—perhaps women use their sense of smell more.

How many different tastes can we detect?

Every food has dissolved molecules that taste buds in your tongue can detect. They send signals to your brain when they pick up one of the main taste sensations: sweet, sour, salty, bitter, and umami (a strong taste in tomatoes, soy sauce, and some cheeses and cooked meats).

YUCK!

Durian fruit

How much difference does smell make?

You might be surprised to learn that nearly three-quarters of what you taste comes from your sense of smell. Your nose detects molecules that give each object its special smell. It sends those signals to the brain, which also picks up the basic taste signals. Without smell, you couldn't distinguish between two different sour, or salty, foods.

What is the worst-smelling food?

One of the most common answers is the Asian fruit known as durian—it smells so bad that it is banned on many buses and trains.

Is pain good for you?

OWWW!

No one likes to feel pain, but without it you'd be in real trouble. That's because pain is the body's alarm system. It's a way of telling you to stop doing something that could be really damaging—like hitting your thumb again with a hammer or walking after you've sprained your ankle.

Is a headache really a pain in your brain?

No. The brain has very few pain receptors so it can't send out pain signals. Most headaches are caused by pain in muscles in your head and neck.

Do some people feel no pain?

Some people—luckily very few—are born unable to feel pain. Their nervous system cannot send those essential warning signals to the brain. Occasionally an illness will cause people to lose their sense of pain, and they run the same risks.

Do we really have a funny bone?

What we call the funny bone—that part of your elbow that gives a zinging feeling when you bang it—is actually a nerve rubbing against a bone in your arm.

Does pain always lead you to a problem spot?

It usually does. You can normally tell which toe you've just stubbed or where someone just poked you with their elbow. But pain around the mouth—especially toothache—can be misleading. The network of nerves in your jaw is so tangled that the problem tooth isn't always near the worst pain.

Why do our moods change?

For years, people were undecided how moods and emotions—feeling happy, sad, or afraid—happened. We now know that they're linked to chemical and electrical changes in our bodies. Things like food, sunshine, exercise, and even our pets can produce those changes.

Why do dogs visit hospitals?

Hospital patients feel happier, but also recover faster, if they have a chance to pat a dog or another pet.

Can sunshine affect your emotions?

When sunlight reaches your skin, your body produces vitamin D, which goes on to produce a happiness hormone called serotonin.

How can running make you happy?

Our bodies constantly produce chemicals called hormones that send messages to the rest of the body. Some of these hormones help us fight disease, and others affect our moods. We can become excited, sad, or happy. Exercise releases some positive hormones that can brighten our mood, which is why people sometimes talk about a "runner's high."

Can doctors measure happiness?

They can measure some of the brain activity that occurs when people are happy. Other specialists can help people relax and examine their own feelings and moods. These relaxed discussions are called therapy, and they help people keep a healthy outlook on life.

Why do we cry?

Crying can be a sign of sadness, but your eyes produce tears in other circumstances, too. Some tears are triggered by our feelings, but others are made every day to wash away dust and other things that shouldn't be in our eyes.

Why do newborn babies cry?

The wailing is the first chance that babies have to get oxygen from the air, rather than from their mother's blood. But they don't produce tears until they are a few weeks old.

Why does crying make your nose run?

Some tears drain into tiny openings in the eyelids and end up inside your nose. You swallow some but others mix with your nasal fluid, making you sniffly. The excess tears spill down your cheeks.

Is there such a thing as a "good cry?"

Scientists have found that the body produces a natural painkiller when we cry, so perhaps crying really does help.

Boo hoo!

Does crying always mean that we're sad?

Other strong emotions—especially sudden happiness—can also make us cry. And because crying is one of the best ways of rinsing, it helps to defend the eyes against painful particles and smells. Just think of how people cry when they cut onions.

Why do you need to sleep?

You spend hours each night—and sometimes during the day—fast asleep, but what is actually going on in your body? Sleep gives our bodies the chance to rebuild, without being constantly on the go. Your muscles grow, tissue gets repaired, and your body is generally restored. It also gives your mind chance to process and store information, ready for the next new day.

What is sleepwalking?

Some people sit up in bed and even get up, walk, and talk while they're still asleep, usually within an hour of falling asleep.

How long should people sleep?

We need less sleep as we get older—starting with about 16 hours a day for babies and down to about nine hours (teenagers) and eventually less than seven hours. Over an average lifetime, you can spend over 200,000 hours—around 23 years—asleep!

Zzzzz..

What makes us wake up?

The cells in your body need more nutrition and oxygen, and they call on you to become active again—so you can eat, and increase your heart rate.

What happens if you go without sleep?

People suffer if they miss a night's sleep, or if their sleep is constantly interrupted. A person could sleep for more than eight hours, but if that sleep is broken they wake up feeling tired. Prolonged sleepless periods can affect people's moods and their physical and mental health.

Does everyone dream?

We all dream when we're asleep. People who think that they don't have dreams simply can't remember them. Dreaming is part of a cycle that goes on each time we fall asleep. And although we know more about dreams, experts still disagree about why we dream... and what dreams mean.

Can some foods give you nightmares?

Eating late, rather than eating particular foods, can disturb your sleep and lead to the type of nasty dream that might wake you—a nightmare.

Can we tell what dreams mean?

It's easy to tell when we're dreaming—our eyes move quickly, even while they're closed. And many people can remember what they dream. But what the dreams mean is harder to say. People once believed that dreams predicted the future. Doctors now admit that they are mysterious, but perhaps a way of sorting out memories.

How long do dreams last?

Some are only a few seconds long, but others can be up to an hour long.

Nerve impulse in brain

What happens when we dream?

Your nightly sleep follows a pattern, or cycle. Much of that is a deep sleep, when the body rebuilds, but several times during the cycle you pass through a period of Rapid Eye Movement (REM). It reflects how active your brain is, as nerve impulses in your brain play out to form dreams.

127

INDEX